Oaksterdam University

Cannabis Terminology Style Guide

2024

First eBook Edition, November 2023

Edited by Angela Bacca, Dale Sky Jones, and Wensdy Von Buskirk
Cover Design by Faith Woodward

Published by Oaksterdam Press
Oakland, California, United States of America

Introduction

More media outlets are reporting on cannabis than ever, requiring common-use definitions of the terms and concepts core to writing about its complexities. Cannabis isn't a simple subject; over 80 years of Prohibition have muddled knowledge of the plant's taxonomy, therapeutic use, cultivation, culture, history, law, and scientific study. There were no common style standards for writing about this subject until this guide was first drafted and edited by the experts at Oaksterdam University in 2022. Cannabis terminology will continue to evolve with use, so we welcome your feedback, input, questions, and requests for clarification as we maintain this resource.

This style guide is designed for use in academia and by any journalist, reporter, writer, or public relations professional. It supplements the AP Style Guide for journalists and PR professionals, and The Chicago Manual of Style for educators.

Adult Use

The term "adult use" is an adjective used to distinguish cannabis use by any person over the age of 21 from those who have a recommendation from a doctor for medicinal use. "Adult use" can and should be used instead of "recreational" because that term is most often associated with activities for children and, therefore, is inappropriate.

See Legalization, Medical/Medicinal, Recreational

Apothecary Style

Also referred to as "deli style"

The "apothecary model" refers to dispensaries that weigh and sell cannabis flower from bulk containers when it is ordered. Although the apothecary model is still used in some regions, most do not allow it. Pre-weighed and packaged flowers are sold in regions that have banned or disallowed this model.

Aeroponics

Like hydroponics, "aeroponics" is a soil-free method of cultivation. Nutrition is provided through fertilizers and supplements mixed into the water. In aeroponics, the plant's roots are suspended in air rather than a soilless growing medium and misted with a nutrient-water solution.

Aeroponics should not be capitalized unless at the beginning of a sentence and defined for unfamiliar audiences at first use.

See Hydroponics

Autoflower
Also referred to as "automatic."
The autoflowering trait in cannabis is a genetic
adaptation that most likely originated in Russia and
Northern China. Autoflowering plants begin their
flowering cycle immediately after germination as
opposed to annual plants that initiate their flowering
cycle in the spring as sunlight hours grow longer.
Autoflowering cannabis plants have shorter life cycles
that benefit cultivators looking to produce multiple
crops outdoors or in climates with short growing
seasons. Indoor cultivators can also benefit from the
quicker maturation cycles of autoflowering cannabis.

European seed banks are most likely to refer to these
varieties as "automatics." Use "autoflower" when
referring to the genetic trait described here and
"automatic" only in varietal names where a company or
nursery already uses it. Depending on the audience,
state that automatic is the same as autoflower and
define it if necessary.
See Indica/Sativa/Ruderalis, Photoperiod

Automatic
See Autoflower

Black Market
See Illegal/Unlicensed/Black Market

Budder ("butter")
See Butane Hash Oil (BHO), Hydrocarbon Extraction

Bud(s)
Also referred to as "flower" or "flowers."

The term "buds" refers to the dried resinous flowers of the cannabis plant, which contain the highest concentrations of THC, CBD, and other desirable phytochemical compounds. The terms "bud" and "flower" are often used in both the plural and the singular in colloquial use. "Bud" should only be used in quotations. Use the term "flowers," plural, since what is referred to alternately as "buds," "bud," or "flower" is actually a cluster of many flowers on a single stem called inflorescences (or racemes).
See Cannabis, Flower(s), Marijuana

Budtender

The term "budtender" is derived from bartender. A budtender is the primary customer service position in a dispensary and helps navigate the wide variety of products available. The use of the term originated in San Francisco Bay Area dispensaries during the early 2000s and is still widely used in most regions, but budtenders are now alternately called patient consultants, retail workers, dispensary associates, or medical cannabis pharmacy agents, depending on regional laws and the preferences of individual dispensaries.
See Dispensary

Butane Hash Oil (BHO)

Also referred to as wax, shatter, budder, and live resin, among many other terms.
Butane hash oil (BHO) is a form of hydrocarbon extraction of cannabis compounds using butane as a solvent. It is not legal to produce BHO at home and is only safe to produce in a licensed facility with professional equipment and trained operators.

BHO is sold in vaporizer cartridges or by the gram for home vaporization or combustion (smoking). It is sold under various names, usually in reference to variations in processing that result in different textures, shades, and consistencies of the finished products. These names include but are not limited to wax, shatter, budder, and live resin.

Spell out "butane hash oil (BHO)" without capitalization at first use and simply "BHO" in every use thereafter. The term BHO does not need to be spelled out on first use if the content audience is familiar. Use the terms "wax," "budder," "shatter," (etc.) only when referencing specific products that use these names.
See Dabs, Extracts, Hydrocarbon Extraction

Cannabimimetic
Cannabimimetic refers to molecular compounds that are not cannabinoids but interact with the endocannabinoid system. Cannabimimetic molecules are found in various plants, including cannabis, frankincense, kava, black pepper, chocolate, echinacea, and liverwort.

Cannabis
Also known as marijuana and hemp
The term "cannabis" refers to any plant in the cannabis genus, including plants grown for their resinous medicinal flowers or industrial uses such as paper, fabric, food, lotions, plastics, and building materials. Cannabis taxonomy is not settled. While the genus *Cannabis* L. is generally agreed upon in scientific communities, species and subspecies are not as clearly

defined. (*See Indica/Sativa/Ruderalis for more clarification on the taxonomy debate.*)

Because of the muddled traditional and legal definitions, reporting on the cannabis and hemp industries also becomes muddled. A common reporting mistake is to refer to hemp as a "cousin" to cannabis or "marijuana." This is inaccurate. Hemp is cannabis but has separate legal and traditional botanical definitions.

The entire cannabis plant — flowers, leaves, seeds, and stalks — is harvestable and usable. Traditionally, plants referred to as "hemp" or "industrial hemp" were bred to harvest their seeds and stalks, which can be manufactured into a long list of byproducts. Plants bred primarily for their resinous flowers, specifically the density of therapeutic compounds they contain, have traditionally been referred to as "marijuana." Legally, it is the overall content of the psychotropic cannabinoid Δ^9-tetrahydrocannabinol (THC) that distinguishes "hemp" from "marijuana." Although the distinction is arbitrary and confuses traditional understandings of cannabis varieties, in the United States, plants that contain less than 0.3% THC are legally considered "hemp," and those that contain greater than 0.3% THC are considered "marijuana" or "cannabis." This arbitrary threshold to distinguish "hemp" from "marijuana/cannabis" ranges from 0.3% to 1% worldwide.

Due to arbitrary THC thresholds, most global and domestic hemp producers focus on low-THC cannabis flowers that contain more significant amounts of cannabidiol (CBD) and other therapeutic compounds instead of growing the plant for its industrial uses.

In most cases, the writer will need to define the terms used in source quotations or legislation. The following definitions allow a writer to assess the meaning of the terms better as they are being used in a particular context and clearly define and clarify them for their audience:

> Hemp can be defined as either:
> - Cannabis flowers grown for non-psychotropic therapeutic compounds, including cannabinoids and terpenes, with an overall THC content arbitrarily set to less than 0.3% in the United States.
> - Cannabis plants grown to harvest their seeds and stalks to make products such as foods, personal care products, fabric, plastics, and sustainable building materials, among many other uses.
>
> Marijuana is defined as:
> - A slang term used to describe the dried resinous flowers of the cannabis plant with a THC content greater than 0.3%.
>
> Cannabis is defined as:
> - The more appropriate term, as opposed to "marijuana," to refer to the dried resinous flowers of the cannabis plant with a THC content greater than 0.3%.
> - The entire plant and all of its uses.

Always default to "cannabis" when referring to what is commonly known as "marijuana." "Marijuana" is a controversial slang term (*See Marijuana*).

When referring to commercial industries, the term "cannabis industry" generally refers to products made from high-THC plants, and "hemp industry" refers to products made from low-THC plants. Again, to provide the reader with the best understanding possible, use the term definitions provided here to clarify the meaning of "hemp" in the context it is being used.

The term "cannabis" should be capitalized and italicized <u>*only*</u> when used in scientific nomenclatures, such as *Cannabis Sativa* L. In all other instances, do not capitalize "cannabis" unless it appears at the beginning of a sentence.
See Cannabinoids, Flowers, Hemp, Marijuana, Reefer Madness

Cannabis Oil
The term "cannabis oil" can refer to any extract or concentrate of cannabis that has an oily consistency but most often refers to full extract cannabis oil (FECO), also known as Rick Simpson Oil (RSO). This term should always be defined clearly for the reader to make the appropriate distinction within the context because it is alternately defined as the following:

- Hemp seed oil
- Carrier oils such as olive or coconut infused with cannabis flowers

- FECO/RSO, which is a dense, thick, tar-like extraction popularized for its therapeutic use by cancer patients
- Distillate oil

See Cannabis, Concentrates, Distillate, Extracts, Full Extract Cannabis Oil (FECO), Hemp, Hydrocarbon Extraction

Cannabinoids
Cannabinoids are compounds that bind to receptors in the endocannabinoid system, which is found in almost all animal life, including humans. There are two main types of cannabinoids: endogenous (originating within the body) and exogenous (originating outside the body).

Endogenous Cannabinoids:
- Endogenous cannabinoids or "endocannabinoids" are produced within the body. Well-known endocannabinoids include anandamide (AEA) and 2-arachidonoylglycerol (2-AG), and others yet to be identified.

Exogenous Cannabinoids:
- Plants produce phytocannabinoids that also interact with the endocannabinoid systems of animals. Cannabis is not the only plant that produces cannabinoids. THC and CBD are (currently) the most commonly sought-after plant-sourced cannabinoids found in the resin of cannabis flowers, yet there are many more.
- "Synthetic cannabinoids" refers to both FDA-approved pharmaceuticals produced in laboratory settings, such as dronabinol

(Marinol®, synthetic THC), and various unregulated "designer" mixtures, like "Spice/K2," which are sold in convenience stores and smoke shops, are dubiously legal, and sometimes dangerous. These do not contain classic cannabinoids, nor do they have the same safety profile.

- Synthesized cannabinoids use chemical processes to convert hemp-sourced cannabinoids such as CBD and THC into THCO, Δ^8-tetrahydrocannabinol (Δ^8-THC), and other cannabinoids that naturally occur in the plant in minimal quantities. Cannabis researchers have raised concerns about their use and safety in new products sold on the hemp market.

While all cannabinoids — endogenous, phyto, synthesized, or synthetic — can be referred to as "cannabinoids," when appropriate within the context of the work, they should be defined to distinguish their source.

Always define "endogenous cannabinoids" at first use and then use "endocannabinoids" for subsequent uses within the same work.

Phytocannabinoids can be referred to in the appropriate context as simply "cannabinoids" because of the common use of the term to refer to THC, CBD, and other cannabis phytocannabinoids. THC and CBD are often referred to as just their acronyms when it is assumed that the audience is already familiar with the terms. While it can be the writer's choice to spell the compounds out fully at first use, the full names of all other cannabinoids should be spelled out before being abbreviated. Here is a list of the most common:

- Δ^9-Tetrahydrocannabinol (THC)
- Cannabidiol (CBD)
- Cannabigerol (CBG)
- Cannabichromene (CBC)
- Cannabinol (CBN)

Always use the delta symbol (Δ) and a superscript 9 with a hyphen in Δ^9-THC and similar compounds. Do not capitalize the full terms unless they appear at the beginning of a sentence.

> Example: Cannabichromene (CBC) and cannabidiol (CBD) are phytocannabinoids.

When using cannabinoids to describe different plant varieties, use a hyphen. In plants, these are referred to as "dominant," and in products, "rich."

> Example: CBD-rich lotion and THC-dominant plants.

If a cannabinoid was synthesized rather than a naturally occurring endo- or phytocannabinoid, state that it is synthetic or synthesized upon first use.

Cannabinoid Acids & Varin Cannabinoids

Before cannabis is heated, compounds such as THC, CBD, and CBG have different molecular forms (they contain an additional carboxyl chain) and are called acid cannabinoids. Always spell them out at first use, and define "acid cannabinoids" if the audience is unlikely to be familiar. The "a" is lowercase in the acronyms. The most common acid cannabinoids and their acronyms are:

- Tetrahydrocannabinolic acid (THCa)
- Cannabidiolic acid (CBDa)
- Cannabigerolic acid (CBGa)

Varin cannabinoids are another form that naturally occur in smaller amounts in some cannabis varieties. The letter "V" remains capitalized in their acronyms:

- Tetrahydrocannabivarin (THCV)
- Cannabidivarin (CBDV)

See Cannabis, Flowers, Hemp

Chemotype/Chemovar
The term "chemotype" classifies cannabis varieties by the spectrum of phytochemicals they produce. The term "chemovar" is a portmanteau for "chemical variety." It classifies plant varieties based on their chemotype or phytochemical profile.
See Genotype, Phenotype

Clone
Cannabis plants are commonly grown from seeds and clones. A clone, or "cutting," is a branch cut from another plant and rooted to grow a new full-sized plant. It has identical genetics to the plant from which it was cut, referred to as "the mother." Define the term at first use for unfamiliar audiences. A simple definition is "starter plant."

Closed-Loop Extraction

Closed-loop extraction refers to making cannabis extracts using volatile solvents (like butane) with industrial equipment. Producing cannabis extractions using volatile solvents is dangerous and should never be done at home. In professional, licensed, and commercial settings, closed-loop extraction machines recycle the solvent rather than disperse it in the air, making the process safer and more sustainable.

Always hyphenate "closed-loop." Do not use "*close* loop."
See Hydrocarbon Extraction, Butane Hash Oil (BHO)

COA

A COA is a laboratory certificate of analysis. Lab testing is required in all commercial cannabis markets, and COAs are the full receipt of these results. They contain potency and safety information such as cannabinoid and terpene content and pesticide and residual solvent testing.

Cola

"Cola" refers to the densest stalk of cannabis flowers at the top of the plant. It is a Spanish word that translates to "tail," referring to the shape resembling a cat's tail. The term came into widespread use in the US during the 1970s, when most cannabis consumed in the US was grown in Mexico. Today, the term is commonly used in the international industry. Do not capitalize unless at the beginning of a sentence or in a formal title.

Combustion
Also referred to as "smoking."
Combustion is a chemical process that creates tar and ash and is the basis for health concerns like bronchitis. The term "combustion" has come into common use in the cannabis industry to differentiate cannabis smoking from cannabis vaporization. In most cases, "combustion" can be used interchangeably with "smoking" if the intended audience is already familiar.

Concentrate
The term "concentrate" refers to the final product of the resinous glands that have been separated from cannabis flowers and concentrated into various forms of hash. As a subcategory of "hash," concentrates are differentiated from "extracts." They are not produced using solvents but through sifting, pressing, rolling, or a combination of agitation and cool temperatures, often ice water. The resulting product is a concentration of the separated resin that can be further subcategorized by the process used to concentrate it. Examples of solventless hash are kief, bubble hash, pressed hash, and rosin. While all extracts are also concentrates, concentrates are not extracts. Unless the audience is familiar with cannabis hashes and subcategories, provide context and a definition at first use.
See Extract, Hash, Kief

Cultivar
The word "strain" is often used to describe varieties of cannabis but is usually used incorrectly. The term "cultivar" is often the more suitable replacement. It is a portmanteau derived from "cultivated variety." It refers to a genetic line of cannabis specifically bred and

selected for the unique and replicable combination of physical traits it will express when grown under specific environmental conditions. Flowers available for sale on dispensary shelves should be referred to as "cultivars." Cultivar can be used instead of "strain" or "variety" where appropriate.

Capitalize cultivar names, which are proper nouns.

> Example: Well-known cultivars include Blue Dream and Grand Daddy Purple.

See Chemotype, Strain, Variety

Cultivation Space
See Garden/Grow/Cultivation Space/Farm

Cultivator
See Gardener/Grower/Farmer/Cultivator

Dab
The term "dab" is used as a noun and a verb. As a verb, it refers to the process of combusting or vaporizing small amounts ("dabs") of extracted cannabis resin. As a noun, it refers to the extracted resins themselves. For clarity, avoid using "dab" and "dabbing" except in quotations or within the appropriate context. Instead, refer to the process of vaporization or cannabis extracts. When using the term, define it at first use unless the primary audience is already familiar with it.
See Butane Hash Oil (BHO), Combustion, Concentrates, Extracts, Hydrocarbon Extraction

Dagga

Dagga is commonly used in South Africa to refer to resinous cannabis flowers (aka "marijuana"). It is a Khoekhoe word, and although English spellings vary, the most widely used and understood is "dagga." Dagga should be defined immediately for international audiences but may not necessarily need a definition for audiences in South Africa.

Deli Style

See Apothecary Style

Dispensary

A dispensary is a brick-and-mortar storefront that is licensed to retail cannabis.

Distillate/Distillation

Cannabis distillate is produced using an extraction method that pulls chemicals out of cannabis resin, concentrates, or other extracts, which results in a refined oil that is almost 100% pure cannabinoids. The process removes terpenes, and while they can be captured and reintroduced, most distillate manufacturers substitute other botanically-derived terpenes. The end product is a subcategory of "extracts" referred to as "distillate." It is produced through the process of "distillation." Unless the audience is already familiar with cannabis extracts, provide context and/or a definition at first use.

See Cannabis Oil, Extracts, Hash, Hydrocarbon Extraction

Drug War/War on Drugs

See War on Drugs

Drug Schedules
Use Roman numerals as opposed to numbers.
Capitalize "Schedule."

> Example: Schedule I, Schedule II, Schedule III,
> Schedule IV, Schedule V

Edibles
The term "edible" refers to any food infused with cannabis. Often, cannabis beverages are legally considered edibles. The term can be defined at first use for unfamiliar audiences as "cannabis-infused food" or "cannabis-infused beverage."

Efficacy
Efficacy describes the use of the substance as "effective" for its intended purposes. Efficacy should not be confused with potency, which describes the quantity of the desired compound within a product.
See Potency

Endocannabinoid System (ECS)
The endocannabinoid system (ECS) is a group of receptors that comprise a complex regulatory system throughout the human brain, body, and central and peripheral nervous systems. Some experts think the endocannabinoid system is the "mother" of all internal systems because it maintains homeostasis by regulating the processes of the body's various systems.

Both naturally-occurring (endogenous or endocannabinoids) and plant-sourced (phytocannabinoids) interact with the ECS to regulate mood, insomnia, pain, digestion, and more. CB1 and CB2 receptors are the most studied and understood. They are found throughout animal bodies regardless of cannabis use. CB1 receptors are primarily found in the central nervous system, and CB2 receptors are found primarily in immune cells.

Do not capitalize "endocannabinoid system" unless it appears at the beginning of a sentence.

Spell out the term at first use and use the acronym ECS for subsequent use.

> Example: All animals have an endocannabinoid system (ECS). The ECS interacts with cannabinoids and other compounds found in plants.

See Cannabinoid

Entourage Effect/Ensemble Effect
The "entourage effect" is a theory postulated in 1999 by Raphael Mechoulam, Ph.D., that the effects of cannabis result from a synergy of all the naturally-occurring plant compounds in cannabis (or other herbs) as opposed to any isolated ingredient within it. Many experts now prefer the term "ensemble effect," which implies harmony among all phytocompounds, as the term "entourage" can imply that one cannabinoid is more important than the others. The terms can be used interchangeably. It is essential to include that the entourage/ensemble effect is a "theory," not settled science.
See Cannabinoid, Flavonoid, Terpene

Extract

An extract is a hash made by stripping cannabis trichomes from plant matter using a chemical solvent such as alcohol, butane, propane, or carbon dioxide. The resulting concentrate is usually no longer considered "full spectrum," except in the case of full extract cannabis oil (FECO), which is considered both an extract and full spectrum. While all extracts are also concentrated, concentrates are not extracts.

The end product of this process is referred to as an extract and is also a type of "hash" further subcategorized by the method used to extract it. Examples of extracted hashes are BHO, live resin, and most oils prepared for personal vaporizer "pens." Unless the audience is already familiar with cannabis hashes and subcategories, provide context and a definition at first use.

See Butane Hash Oil (BHO), Concentrates, Distillate, Hash, Hydrocarbon Extraction

Fan Leaves

The term "fan leaves" refers to the larger leaves that grow from the cannabis stem and branches to collect sunlight to fuel the process of photosynthesis. The five-fingered fan leaf is also the symbol most commonly associated with the cannabis plant. Terms such as "shade leaves" and "primary leaves" can be used interchangeably as long as the meaning is clear in context to the reader.

Farm

See Garden/Grow/Cultivation Space/Farm

Farmer
See Gardener/Grower/Farmer/Cultivator

Flavonoid
Flavonoids are color pigments found in cannabis and other plants with known medicinal properties. They are part of what is referred to as the "full spectrum" of cannabis compounds found in "whole plant" cannabis products. Cannabis contains common flavonoids with known therapeutic properties found in other plants, such as quercetin and luteolin, and cannflavins, which are unique to the cannabis plant.
See Full Spectrum, Whole Plant

Flower(s)
Also referred to as "bud" or "buds."
The term "flowers" refers to the resinous reproductive floral structures of the cannabis plant. These flowers have the highest concentration of resin, which contains THC, CBD, and other desirable chemical compounds.

The term "flower" is often used in both the plural and singular in colloquial use. The most accurate term to use is "flowers," plural, because rather than being a single flower, what is referred to alternately as "buds," "bud," or "flower" is actually inflorescences (or racemes), which is a cluster of flowers on a single stem.
See Bud(s), Cannabis, Marijuana

Full Extract Cannabis Oil (FECO)/Rick Simpson Oil (RSO)/Cannabis Oil
When made correctly, full extract cannabis oil (FECO) is a highly concentrated extract that includes as much of

the full spectrum of phytocompounds as possible. It is thick, black, tar-like, and highly concentrated. It was popularized for use in cancer and other chronic or fatal illnesses by Canadian cancer patient Rick Simpson. Simpson popularized original methods for home production, and the resulting oil was referred to as Rick Simpson Oil (RSO). West Coast growers began preparing the oil using food-grade alcohol solvents and refer to the resulting product as FECO in the 2010s.

Unless appropriate in the context, use the term full extract cannabis oil (FECO) rather than Rick Simpson Oil (RSO). Rick Simpson Oil is always capitalized because it is a proper noun. Full extract cannabis oil is not capitalized unless at the beginning of a sentence. Spell out at first use and then use the acronyms thereafter for both terms.

The term "cannabis oil" is vaguely used to refer to FECO, RSO, and many other cannabis-infused oils and should always be defined for clarity.
See Cannabis Oil, Extracts

Full Spectrum
Full spectrum refers to the entirety of the phytochemical compounds found in cannabis. Do not hyphenate.
See Whole Plant.

Ganja
Ganja is the term used in Jamaica and India to refer to dried resinous cannabis flowers. Only use this term in quotations or the relevant context of the cultural history of the plant in Jamaica and India.

Garden/Grow/Cultivation Space/Farm

While the terms are often used interchangeably in colloquial use, the terms distinguish size and market.

- "Garden" refers to small-scale cultivation, usually by a home grower/gardener.
- "Farm" refers to larger-scale outdoor cultivation.
- "Cultivation space" can refer to indoor or outdoor cultivation of any size but is most appropriately used for indoor spaces.
- The terms "grow," "grow operation," or "grow op" have traditionally been used as nouns and are associated with the legacy/illegal market. Do not use these terms unless in quotations or the appropriate historical context.

The terms "garden" and "farm" are often used as verbs and should remain consistent with the terms defined here as nouns.

Gardener/Grower/Farmer/Cultivator

The choice of the term should be consistent with the noun used to reference the garden, grow, farm, or cultivator. Although "grow op" or "grow" is a legacy market term that may no longer be appropriate, "grower" is appropriate for any cultivator.
See Garden/Grow/Farm/Cultivation Space

Genotype

Genotype is a term used to classify cannabis varieties strictly by genetics.
See Chemotype, Phenotype

Grow
See Garden/Grow/Cultivation Space/Farm

Grower
See Gardener/Grower/Farmer/Cultivator

Hash/Hashish
"Hash" is a catch-all term for all extractions or concentrations of the resins produced by cannabis flowers. The "hash" type should be defined for clarity unless used in a quotation. There are many options, with the most common being:

- "Hashish" is an Arabic term that refers to pressed cannabis resin produced using traditional methods, such as sifting. The term should only refer to this traditional product made using traditional methods or in the appropriate historical and cultural context. No solvents are used to produce hashish.
- "Solventless hash" is a catch-all term for modern concentrated cannabis resin produced without using a chemical solvent, such as sifting, water extraction, or pressing. Types of solventless hash include "bubble hash" and "rosin." Solventless is different from "solvent-free," which implies a chemical solvent (like butane) was used but has been properly purged to non-detectable levels.
- Hydrocarbon extractions such as butane hash oil (BHO).

See Butane Hash Oil (BHO), Concentrates, Extracts, Hydrocarbon Extraction

Hemp

Although "cannabis" and "hemp" are regulated separately, hemp is, in fact, also cannabis. Traditionally, plants referred to as "hemp" or "industrial hemp" were bred to harvest their seeds and stalks, which can be manufactured into a long list of byproducts. Plants bred for their leaves and resinous flowers, specifically the density of therapeutic compounds they contain, have traditionally been referred to as "marijuana." Legally, it is the overall content of the psychotropic cannabinoid Δ^9-tetrahydrocannabinol (THC) that distinguishes "hemp" from "marijuana." Although the distinction is arbitrary and confuses traditional understandings of cannabis varieties, plants that contain less than 0.3% THC are legally considered "hemp" in the United States, and those that contain greater than 0.3% THC are considered "marijuana" or "cannabis."

With the legalization of hemp, the 0.3-1% THC threshold has shifted the majority of the global and domestic "hemp" markets toward producing low-THC cannabis flowers rather than growing the plant for its industrial uses.

Because of the muddled traditional and legal definitions, reporting on the hemp industry also becomes muddled. Common reporting mistakes include referring to hemp as "the male plants" or as a "cousin" to cannabis or "marijuana." Neither assertion is accurate. Hemp is cannabis.

In most cases, the writer will need to define the terms used in source quotations and legislation. The following definitions allow a writer to assess the meaning of the terms better as they are being used in a particular context and clearly define them for their audience:

Hemp can be defined as either:

- Cannabis flowers that are grown for their non-psychotropic therapeutic compounds, including cannabinoids and terpenes, with an overall THC content of less than 0.3% THC (in the United States, up to 1% in other countries).
- Cannabis plants that are grown for their seeds and stalks to make products such as foods, personal care products, fabric, plastics, and sustainable building materials, among many other uses.

When referring to the industry, the term "cannabis industry" generally refers to products made from high-THC plants, and "hemp industry" refers to products made from low-THC plants but can sometimes instead refer to traditional industrial uses. Again, to provide the reader with the best understanding possible, use the term definitions provided here to clarify the meaning of "hemp" in the context it is being used.
See Cannabis, Marijuana

Hydrocarbon Extract
"Hydrocarbon extract" refers to hashes extracted with hydrocarbon solvents such as butane, ethanol, or propane. The end products are referred to as butane

hash oil (BHO), ethanol hash oil (EHO), or propane hash oil (PHO), respectively. The techniques used to produce each subcategory of hydrocarbon-extracted hash varies.

Home or DIY production of hydrocarbon extracts is dangerous. They are only safe to produce in a legal, licensed setting with well-trained staff and professional industrial equipment.

Hydrocarbon extracts are sold by the gram, a half gram, or in vaporizer cartridges under various names, usually in reference to variations in processing that result in different textures, shades, and consistencies of the finished products. These names include but are not limited to wax, live resin, shatter, taffy, pull and snap, sugar, budder, and batter/badder.

If the audience is already familiar with variations of hash and hydrocarbon extracts, there is no need to define terms. If the audience is unfamiliar, use the definitions here to provide relevant clarification and context.
See Butane Hash Oil (BHO), Concentrates, Dabs, Extracts

Hydroponics
Hydroponics is a method of plant cultivation where nutrition is provided through water in a soilless medium.
See Aeroponics

Illegal/Unlicensed/Black Market

Although the term "black market" refers to unlicensed/illegal markets, the term is offensive and should not be used. Instead, refer to the market as "illegal," "illicit," "unregulated," or "unlicensed." In the case of the semi-legal medical cannabis markets on the West Coast before adult use legalization, these markets should be referred to as "the legacy market." "Legacy" should only refer to the operators who originated safe access for medical patients and should not be used interchangeably with violent criminal cartels.

See Legacy Market

Indica/Sativa/Ruderalis

The terms "indica," "sativa," and "ruderalis" refer to different subtypes of cannabis based on their geographic origins and common traits. While "indica" and "sativa" are commonly used to describe the effects of varieties — such as indicas produce sedative effects, and sativas produce stimulating effects — this is inaccurate. Only use these terms in quotations to describe effects, adding clarification to correct inaccuracies. The terms are appropriately used to categorize plants by origin and common traits. Although the term "ruderalis" has not taken on the same meanings as "indica" and "sativa," it is yet another subtype of cannabis defined by geographic origin and common traits:

- Indicas originated in the Hindu Kush mountain range and tend to be smaller, denser, darker green, have thicker leaf blades, and begin flowering earlier than sativa plants.

- Sativas evolved in equatorial regions and tend to be taller, looser, lighter green, have thinner leaf blades, and begin flowering later than indica plants.

- Ruderalis plants originated in Northern Russia are smaller and contain the "autoflowering" trait, meaning they automatically begin flowering shortly after germination and mature quickly, regardless of the season.

Most plants cultivated in modern markets are hybrid varieties bred from a mix of these varieties.

Only capitalize these terms at the beginning of a sentence. Italicize only when used in scientific nomenclature. In all other instances, do not capitalize or italicize.

A note on the taxonomy debate:

There will be more nuance to using these classifications for those writing for scientific audiences or audiences familiar with the taxonomy debate. Over the years, various other taxonomies have been proposed. The majority are divided into two camps: the "lumpers" (who lump cannabis into as few categories as possible) and the "splitters," who feel there are more species or other species than are currently recognized. Karl Hillig and Robert Clarke view hemp plants as "sativas" and lump all other plants into indica sub-species. In 2015, Robert McPartland proposed a new taxonomy based on geographic origin, where "sativa" would now be indica (because they originated in India), and "indica" would become afghanica (because these plants originated in Afghanistan), and "ruderalis" would be "sativa." Most people adhere to the old indica, sativa, and ruderalis framework, but it is subject to change as new research comes in.

See Cannabis, Hemp

Joint

A joint is a slang term for pre-rolled cannabis cigarettes.

See Pre-Roll

Kief

Kief refers to the sifted trichomes (resin) of dried cannabis flowers. It is smoked, added to foods, or processed into hashes.

See Hash, Trichomes

Legacy Market

The term "legacy grower" is often used to distinguish pre-legalization multi-generational cultivators from illicit production associated with environmental degradation and violent crime. The term often implies support for early advocacy movements, the use of sustainable and organic practices, and association with popularizing many well-known cannabis cultivars, but it is open to interpretation and individual perceptions due to its loose use in marketing. Writers should define it at first use.

Legalization, Decriminalization & Descheduling

The terms "legalization," "decriminalization," and "descheduling" are often used similarly, but they each have distinct meanings. While they all describe changes to current law, each is a distinct policy change:

- Legalization is when a jurisdiction authorizes, regulates, or otherwise permits cannabis use, possession, and commercial activities.
- Decriminalization is not legalization but removal or significant reduction of criminal or legal penalties associated with personal cannabis use and possession. Under most state-level decriminalization schemes, civil penalties/fines remain in place.
- Descheduling means completely removing cannabis from the Controlled Substances Act of 1970. Drug scheduling happens at the state and federal levels, so true "descheduling" would have to happen federally and state-by-state. The President, Congress, and the DEA can change this federal designation.

Live Resin

Live resin is a hydrocarbon extraction of fresh, usually frozen cannabis flowers that were not cured or dried. Live resins generally have more terpenes (scent molecules). Live resin is not capitalized unless at the beginning of a sentence. For unfamiliar audiences, clarify that it is a type of cannabis hash extraction at first use.

See Butane Hash Oil (BHO), Extracts, Hydrocarbon Extraction

Marijuana (also Marihuana)

The term "marijuana" refers to the dried resinous flowers of the cannabis plant. The modern use of the term originated in Northern Mexico and was popularized in American culture through racist anti-Mexican propaganda. "Marijuana" is a controversial term today because of its use to create this negative association leading up to Prohibition.

Although it is written into many federal and state laws, it is not scientifically accurate. It is believed this negative association was used to obscure that "marijuana" is cannabis and garner support for prohibiting a "scary new drug" coming across the US-Mexico border.

The term should only be used in quotations or the appropriate historical or cultural context. There are several theories of the word's original etymology, as the plant did not appear to exist in the pre-Columbian Americas.

Marijuana was alternately spelled "marihuana" during the time of the Marihuana Tax Act (1937). Only use this spelling in the appropriate historical context. When writing about law, the writer must use the same terminology, usually "marijuana," increasingly "cannabis," and less often "marihuana." Both "marijuana" and "marihuana" can be used appropriately in a sentence.

See Cannabis, Flower(s)

Measurements
From the 1940s to the 1970s, most of the cannabis consumed in the United States was purchased from other countries that use the metric system, and it was therefore sold in metric units: kilograms and grams. There are 1,000 grams in a kilogram, and a gram was a popular unit of measurement for small purchases. With the rise of domestic cultivation, cannabis in the United States is now sold in a blend of metric and imperial units: pounds, ounces, *and* grams. In the United States, units of cannabis flowers are sold under the following terms:

- Pound (16 ounces)
- Ounce (approximately 28 grams)
- "Quarter" (one-quarter of an ounce, approximately 7 grams)
- "Eighth" (one-eighth of an ounce, approximately 3.5 grams)
- "Tenth"* (one-tenth of an ounce, approximately 2.8 grams)
- Gram

The "tenth" is only a measurement under state law in Ohio, where "eighths" are not sold in licensed dispensaries.

Medical/Medicinal
Although they have distinct meanings, "medical" and "medicinal" are often used interchangeably. Most state laws refer to "medical" marijuana or cannabis, so this term must be used when referring to legislation or the category of the commercial market.

The term "medical" refers specifically to the practice of medicine by the medical industry, and "medicines" are FDA-approved pharmaceuticals and over-the-counter drugs.

The term "medicinal" is an adjective used to describe substances with properties of therapeutic value. Cannabis in its natural form does not fit the definition of a "medicine," but the purpose of consumption is often therapeutic. Therefore, the term "medicinal" is more appropriate to describe the therapeutic use of cannabis.
See Adult Use

N-P-K
N-P-K stands for nitrogen (N), phosphorus (P), and potassium (K). N-P-K are "macronutrients" because they are the primary nutrients most plants require for growth. These three elements' ratios are prominently displayed on all plant fertilizers and nutritional supplement labels. Different plants have different nutritional needs at different stages of the life cycle. Because the term is a ratio displayed in numbers such as 6-4-4, "N-P-K" is also hyphenated.
See Aeroponics, Hydroponics

Phenotype/Pheno Hunt
Cannabis is primarily dioecious, meaning there are separate male and female plants. As a result, breeding cannabis is relatively simpler than many other plants and can be done by amateurs and dedicated breeders alike. When two plants are bred, the resulting seeds inherit genes from the parent plants but, like human siblings, are unique from one another.

The term "phenotype" refers to different distinguishable traits between plants. These traits include plant height, yield, leaf size, the spectrum of phytochemicals, and more. Only use this term in the context of plant genetics. A "pheno hunt" is a term used by cultivators to describe the process of germinating multiple seeds of one variety to select specific plants that express the desired traits.

Photoperiod
Cannabis plants are summer annuals, meaning they evolved to germinate in the spring, begin growing flowers after the summer solstice, and ripen in the fall. Annual plants respond to the ratio of darkness to light and other seasonal shifts in temperature and moisture. They measure when the nights become progressively longer to initiate and complete the flower production process. The term "photoperiod" refers to this ratio of darkness to light. Different varieties of cannabis have slightly different photoperiod requirements to trigger flowering. Indoors, the grower controls the photoperiod to mimic this environmental trigger.
See Autoflower

Pot
Because this slang term is almost always used in a derogatory way to refer to "cannabis flowers," do not use it unless in a quotation or the appropriate cultural or historical context.
See Buds, Cannabis, Marijuana

Potency
Potency refers to the concentration of a desired compound within a product, as opposed to efficacy, which refers to the effectiveness of a product for its intended use. *See Efficacy*

Pre-Roll
A pre-roll is a pre-rolled joint.
See Joint

Prescription/Recommendation
Because cannabis is a Schedule I drug, it cannot be prescribed in the United States and most of the world. The term "prescription" is often incorrectly used in reference to suggested use by a doctor. Doctors write letters of recommendation where the medicinal use of cannabis is legal. FDA-approved pharmaceutical synthetic cannabinoid medicines (like Marinol®) and botanically-derived cannabinoid medicines (like Epidiolex®) are prescribed rather than recommended.

Prohibition
The term "Prohibition" refers to banning any drug, substance, or behavior. Do not capitalize it unless it is at the beginning of a sentence, in a formal title, or referring to a specific prohibition, such as alcohol or cannabis. In writings where it is obvious to the audience that "Prohibition" only means cannabis Prohibition, the term "cannabis" is an unnecessary qualifier.

Psychotropic/Psychoactive
Although the term "psychoactive" has come to be understood as feeling "high," the term "psychotropic" is the correct term to use in this context. While the words

have similar meanings, "psychotropic" is defined as "affecting mental activity, behavior, or perception" or the feeling of "being high."

"Psychoactive" is defined as a substance that affects mental processes. CBD affects neurological conditions such as epilepsy and is, therefore, "psychoactive." It is non-psychotropic. Do not use the term "non-psychoactive" to refer to phytochemicals from cannabis that do not produce the "high" associated with THC. Instead, use "non-psychotropic." Using a strict definition of psychoactivity, chocolate, coffee, tobacco, and many other substances are also considered psychoactive.

Recreational
Although the term "recreational" is commonly used to refer to the use of cannabis by adults who do not have a doctor's recommendation, the more appropriate term is "adult use." "Adult use" can and should be used in place of "recreational" because the term is most often associated with activities for children.
See Adult Use, Legalization, Medical/Medicinal

Reefer Madness
The title of the 1936 movie *Reefer Madness* is often used to describe any anti-cannabis rhetoric or propaganda considered extreme or derogatory. Always capitalize "Reefer Madness" and use quotation marks in this context, even if not explicitly referencing the film. Defer to Chicago or AP Style when referencing the film.

Rick Simpson Oil (RSO)
See Full Extract Cannabis Oil (FECO)

Ruderalis
See Indica/Sativa/Ruderalis

Sativa
See Indica/Sativa/Ruderalis

Screen of Green
A screen of green is a cultivation term that describes the manipulation of leaves and branches with netting so the plant canopy receives as much light as possible in an indoor garden. Spell out the term at first use and abbreviate it thereafter as "ScrOG." This formatting of the acronym is from the traditional use of the term in cannabis-centric publications.

Science/Studies
Be careful not to report the results of a single study as fact. Always review the study's methodology and see if other research has replicated or supported the results. Do not use titles such as "science says," as "science" cannot "say."

Another common mistake is to report on preclinical cannabis studies done in labs with isolated cannabis compounds and human cells (or in animal models) as definitive. Although these studies are a sound basis for future research, their results do not necessarily extrapolate to actual diverse human use with diverse natural plants.

Seed-to-Sale
Seed-to-sale refers to the regulatory chain of custody, most often used to refer to the software required by state laws and federal guidelines that track medical and adult use cannabis supply chains. Always hyphenate seed-to-sale.

Shatter
See BHO

Sinsemilla
The term "sinsemilla" means "without seed" in Spanish. It refers to unfertilized cannabis that results in larger, more resinous flowers rather than seeds. Its use was popularized through cultivation in Mexico in the 1970s and is not currently a common use term and should only be used in quotations or the appropriate historical or cultural context.

Solvent
"Solvent" refers to substances that separate cannabinoids, terpenes, and flavonoids from the leaves to produce cannabis extracts. Common solvents include alcohol, butane, and carbon dioxide.
See Butane Hash Oil (BHO), Extracts, Hash, Hydrocarbon Extraction

Strain
See Cultivar, Chemotype, Variety, Indica/Sativa/Ruderalis

Terpene
Terpenes are aroma molecules found in cannabis and other plants. Terpenes have known medicinal

properties. They are part of what is referred to as the "full spectrum" of cannabis compounds found in "whole plant" cannabis products. Terpenes deter pests in living plants, are found in many other plants, and have a wide range of known therapeutic utility.

It has become common in places where cultivation is legal for the media to report on odor complaints near cannabis cultivation sites and repeat commentary, through quotations or otherwise, that inhaling cannabis terpenes is potentially dangerous for the communities where it is cultivated. While the smell may bother some, the terpenes found in cannabis are no different than those found in all other cultivated crops and plants found in nature and should be treated similarly. Seek expert commentary and clarification when engaging in this sort of reporting.
See Flavonoids, Full Spectrum, Whole Plant

THC
Δ^9-Tetrahydrocannabinol (THC) is the most abundantly found phytocannabinoid in cannabis.
See Cannabis, Cannabinoids, Hemp

Tincture
A tincture is a liquid extraction or infusion of cannabis sold in dropper bottles for easy dosing. It is often made with alcohol, glycerin, olive, or coconut oil. Tinctures are usually administered sublingually (under the tongue) for quick absorption, but they can also be used topically or in cooking. The term "tincture" is not capitalized unless at the beginning of a sentence or in a specific product name.

Topicals
"Topicals" refers to products infused with cannabis applied to the skin for various therapeutic or cosmetic uses.

Trichome
Trichomes are resinous glands that grow on cannabis plants, mainly the flowers, containing high concentrations of cannabinoids, terpenes, flavonoids, and other phytochemicals with therapeutic properties. They are sometimes stripped from the plant to create concentrates or removed using a solvent to produce extractions.
See Concentrate, Cannabinoid, Extract, Flavonoid, Hash, Terpene

Variety/Varietal
The term "variety" or "varietal" is a blanket term that can refer to any different type of cannabis plant and is an acceptable alternative to "strain." Variety names are proper nouns and should be capitalized.
See Cultivar, Chemotype, Indica/Sativa/Ruderalis, Strain

War on Drugs/Drug War
The "War on Drugs" is a proper noun and should be capitalized, similar to other declared wars such as The Vietnam War or World War II. It is America's longest war.

When the term "Drug War" refers to the War on Drugs, it is capitalized as another form of that proper title. The Drug War and War on Drugs can be used interchangeably at the writer's discretion. When referring to any nonspecific war involving drugs, no capitalization is required.

Wax
See BHO

Whole Plant
Whole plant is not hyphenated and can be used interchangeably with "full spectrum."
See Full Spectrum.

Need fact-checking or experts to review your content before you publish?

Oaksterdam University is happy to review your content for accuracy and provide quotes from authoritative experts and specialists from every facet of the cannabis industry. Please contact media@oaksterdamuniversity.com for assistance.

Made in the USA
Middletown, DE
07 November 2023